THE SECOND
SPARKY BOOK
OF HOURS

Father Claus

I wish you luck and Christmas cheer,
I wish you'd leave me cheese this year.
Mince pies and sherry are the biz,
But Santa tells me these are his.
Yet why he eats without his beard,
We all agreed was very weird.

THE SECOND
SPARKY®
BOOK OF HOURS

BY

LUCIAN EYERS

Illustrated by the Author

E'mage

Published by E'mage 2008
Text and Illustrations © Lucian Eyers 2008

Hardback Edition

E'mage © Registered Trade Mark

SPARKY © Registered Trade Mark

Registration in the U.S. Patent and Trade Mark Office

A CIP catalogue record for this book is available
from the British Library.

ISBN 978 1 898501 11 4
EAN 9781898501114

Printed and bound in England by
TJ International Ltd, Padstow, Cornwall

Other Sparky titles can be found at:
www·sparky·co·uk
www.thesparkybookofhours.com

Being Tall

I do declare in front of all,
There's more to life than being tall.
I stood on boxes, sat in trees,
Whilst others stared bemused at me.

The rush of power didn't stay,
Instead most people turned away.
And though this may be no surprise,
I'd rather see those telling eyes.

A note to the reader

If I was thus a modest man,
I'd say about this book,
If you have nothing much to do,
This could be worth a look.

But if my mind allowed me,
For a second to be proud,
I'd say to everyone I see,
Please read this book out loud.

The truth is sired from my desire,
To shed a little light.
And if these words won't resonate,
Another day they might.

Lucian Eyers

Contents

Autumn's Come

A mist lies on the sodden land,
It passes over beast and man,
And breathes on leaves of yellow, red,
While morning's tears suspend from web.

Dark waters flow from mossy ledge,
Ripe berries fall from sumptuous hedge.
The bounty of this parting song,
I hear so clear – the autumn's come.

Patricia's Progress

Patricia's now a pretty thing,
  With kindly eyes and golden wings.
And so to keep you up to date,
Patricia's looking for a mate.

The reason why she's still alone,
Patricia never leaves her home,
While queues of handsome, desperate drakes,
Wait patiently outside her gate.

"My dear Patricia don't be shy,
You'll never know until you try,
That I can be the one for you,"
Is heard disturbing morning's dew.

The Dragonfly

Until today I can't deny,
 I'd never met a dragonfly.
The ugly picture in my head,
Was lashing teeth and spindly legs.

A mutant with a violent tongue,
Just burning homes and eating dung.
Great scaly back with stubby wings,
The cursed fiend a nightmare brings.

On meeting Mr. Dragonfly,
I found him quite a pleasant guy.
Incased with jewels and crystal wings,
An undisputed insect king.

And so I have decided to,
Be cautious when I form my view.
For what will occupy our minds,
In truth, is rarely what we find.

The Kingfisher

He could not know what lurked below,
Where murky currents gently flow.
The cunning eye of sabred beast,
Lay waiting for his royal feast.

The pike was angry, sad and mean,
The bird a lovely shade of green.
For there he sat on twig of birch,
Surveying silver backs of perch.

His friends sung disapproving songs,
"To leap in blind is simply wrong.
There could be anything in there,"
Was heard by pike with greedy stare.

Then silver skin of dace appeared,
As turquoise feathers disappeared,
And great commotion filled the stream,
While feathered folk began to scream.

"The pike has caught the little bird,
There's nothing we can do," was heard.
"The seething monster's teeth are red,
As bird lies on a sandy bed."

But still the fighting soldiered on,
Until the pike had finally gone.
And resting on a mossy bank,
A tired bird with luck to thank.

For few can tell such fishing tales,
When how his beak did spear the tail,
Of giant beast ten times his size,
And for his courage still survive.

Not always can we see or touch,
Those things in life that matter much.
When courage is for you a must,
Then all you need to do is trust.

My Dearest Tree

"My dearest tree, it's only me,
I'd like a quiet word.
In all your great experience,
How best do God I serve?

Should I have been a prophet,
Or help others with their health?"
"The only service you must learn,
Is how to be yourself."

"That seems to be too easy,
And besides I've often tried.
But sadly being me involves,
Much anger, hate and pride."

"You need to be, 'the best in you,'
And understand your worth.
For you were made of goodness,
Long before you walked this earth.

You may believe you're sinful,
Only learning to be good.
But this is not the way it is,
So change this view, you should.

Remember then from whence you came,
And you will be inspired.
Almighty God is in us all,
And badness you've acquired."

Part II

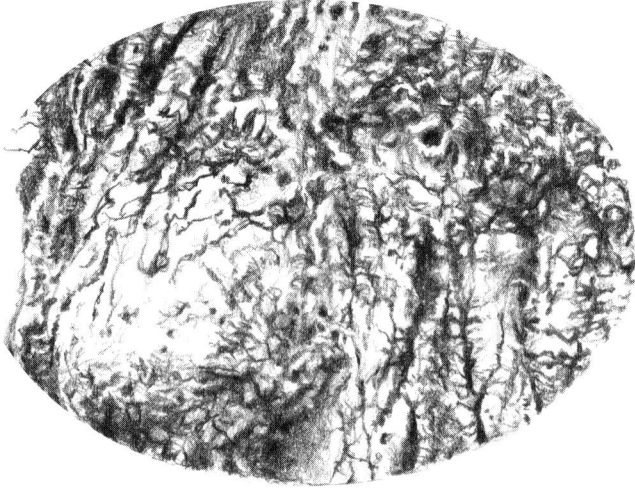

"Tread gently on my mossy bed,
   And stroke my bark with gentleness.
And ask yourself what you can feel,
Or does this seem to feel unreal?"

"It does feel strange for now I view,
What complex bark God's given you.
The tiny threads of matted web,
The beauty of your peacefulness.

I thank you tree for letting me,
Enjoy a world I never see."

Part III

"It would be nice to be like you,
Oh wise and kindly tree.
What can I do, so I improve,
The qualities in me?"

"What is it then you see in me,
That you would like to be?
For though my years are very long,
To most I'm just a tree."

"Your patience is immeasurable,
And few are quite so beautiful,
And though the weather taunts you,
You remain so still and strong."
"Then keep that rooted in your heart,
And seldom you'll go wrong."

Jamie's Basket

Sweet Jamie's been a busy man,
Providing for a handsome clan.
Today I counted twenty two,
Rewards for all his I love yous.

He says he loves them all the same,
But can't remember any names.
And though he rarely seems to whine,
The day provides him little time.

With thoughts of Jamie's happiness,
This very subject I addressed.
"My friend, your basket's full to brim,
There's no more room to put them in.

Can I suggest you take things slow,
For prudence comes with saying – no,
And thus avoid a crowded nest.
Besides, you seem to need the rest."

Dear Daphne

Daphne saved my life today,
  A debt that's very hard to pay.
Outnumbered by a gruesome crew,
The valiant wings of Daphne flew,
And swooped amongst fierce teeth and claws,
While others watched behind closed doors.

Both tired and bruised but still alive,
I asked dear Daphne what she'd like.
"What can I give for all your help?"
She said, "Do this for someone else."

The Scarecrow

They teased him 'til December's snow,
Embraced his rags with silver glow.
"A snowman you shall be tonight,"
The winter laughed in strange delight.

By morning Scarecrow looked his best,
As crows vacated cosy nests,
To find the subject of their scorn,
Had suffered such, he'd finally gone.

"I never can forgive myself,
Perhaps we caused undue bad health,"
Was on the beak of every crow,
As guilty seeds began to sow.

That night each crow did swear a pledge,
While perched upon a frosted hedge:
"No longer will we taunt your name,
Dear Scarecrow, please return again."

And so the wind and rain that night,
Left Scarecrow in the morning light,
Just as he was before the snow,
Amongst a jubilant flock of crows.

Two lessons I have learnt today,
To send me on my merry way:
Appreciation's often found,
By others when you're not around.

And though a crow may seem annoyed,
It could be he is overjoyed.

Looking for an Angel

An angel on our Christmas tree,
Would be so very nice to see.
And so he left for many hours,
Returning late with only flowers.

One lady said, "We've all sold out,"
Another said, "There's little doubt,
That last year we had quite a few,
But with this star, you could make do."

They tried to sell me all they had,
And must have thought I'm raving mad.
Synthetic fairies, sparkling frogs,
Were just a few they tried to flog.

I did the very best I could,
I even looked for one in wood.
I just can't find one any where,
And so they left the tree top bare.

Talking to your Angel

He asked me how to do it,
I said, "It's up to you.
Talking to your angel,
Is just how I talk to you.

But don't forget to thank them,
For answering your prayers,
And try to be specific,
In your worries or your cares.

Talking to your angel,
Is listening with your heart.
But this will only happen,
If you make a conscious start."

"But who is actually talking,
Is not easily understood."
"The devil's plans are always bad,
An angel's voice is good.

Talking to your angel,
Is just part of daily life.
Like talking to your brother,
Or your mother or your wife."

"It's really not that easy,"
He anxiously replied.
"I've listened and I've chattered,
But there's nothing when I've tried."

"The tiniest of messages,
Will be how they respond.
A word or sign upon your mind,
Will show you right from wrong."

But even more excited,
And frustrated he became.
"There's nothing you have said to me,
That helps me to relay."

"Communication's only heard,
When you are at your best.
So this means being very calm,
And trust will do the rest."

Death of an Angel

When he was only five years old,
  The dearest angel died.
And though he laughed and smiled so much,
My brother never cried.

They laid him on a marble slab,
So pale and still he slept.
And at his feet, so great was he,
That seven children wept.

His coffin seemed so small,
And meagre for a child,
Who gave so very much to us,
And touched so many lives.

But that was many years ago,
For now I am a man.
Yet why a child should leave so soon,
I now do understand.

My brother was an angel,
And his goodness fell on ears,
That needed much encouragement,
Though difficult the years.

He taught me love is generous,
Asked for nothing in return.
And though his voice was never heard,
How much we seemed to learn.

When death decides to take a child,
It's hard to comprehend.
But this will often mean a cherub's
Waiting to ascend.

If I'd known then, my brother's soul,
Had planned so little years,
The pain we shared amongst ourselves,
Would shed so fewer tears.

"Don't cry for me," I hear him say,
"For now you understand,
That I am watching over you,
To help you all I can."

Grow

You may remember meeting,
    Mrs. Moorhen and her young.
But now her work is over,
Mrs. Moorhen wants some fun.

"More hens, more work are not for me,
More sleep, more food, more breaks.
For what's the point of life," she said,
"To give and not to take?"

The reason why we're here at all,
She really didn't know.
"No need to lie," I thus replied,
"We're on this earth to grow.

Of course you may believe our souls,
Do simply not exist.
So think before you later find,
The point of life you've missed."

A moment's silence followed,
As the moorhen chose her words.
"Please tell me how my soul can grow,
I'm just a stupid bird?"

"In saying that my little friend,
You've made a mighty leap.
The rest will come with patience,
And a will you can succeed.

The tests in life that stunt your growth,
Are hatred, worry, greed.
But kindness, trust and generous love,
Will give you all you need."

The moorhen was excited,
"Well, this news is really great.
I'll never lie and rarely sigh,
At anyone I hate."

"There's something else I wish to say,
You haven't got there yet.
For sadly what we learn today,
Tomorrow – we forget."

Acts of God

There are such things as acts of God,
  But here's the big surprise,
Just what we do upon this earth,
Reflects upon the sky.

A lightning burst at very worst,
Will strike what it can see.
So stay away from angry words,
Nor shelter under tree.

There are such things as acts of God,
But God won't interfere.
Yet what of famine, fire and floods?
Bears heavy on my ears.

On Thursday morning, 9am,
The President decreed,
"The starving millions on this earth,
We can no longer feed.

Instead the fight on evil men,
Must be our common aim."
But by next morning on his land,
The floods and famine came.

For fighting only fuels a fear,
That some may choose to keep.
Yet food will prove we paid the price,
So children may not weep.

I understand confusion may,
Be clouding up your mind.
Just when it's God and when it's not,
Is hard to thus define.

Just don't assume He's angry,
When the lightning strikes above.
The key to solve this puzzle is,
Remember, God is love.

There's consequence in all we do,
And all we do will tell,
If on this earth we live in peace,
Or die in living Hell.

Clarissa Said

I have been told but can't say how,
Clarissa is a lazy cow.
An appetite beyond compare,
Concerned with only her affairs.

A selfish beast who's often cold,
Is how Clarissa's story's told.
And so before a fading light,
I crept to see just who was right.

But every madam looked the same,
And no one dared to give their name.
But as I left, I heard a yelp!
"Good evening Miss and may I help?"

"I'm looking for another cow,"
But said, "It doesn't matter now."
We talked until the sun went red,
While others turned to meadow's bed.

I told her of my quest to find,
If branded words were truth or lies.
She asked me what this would achieve,
Her tone was that she disagreed.

"For then," I said, "I'll truly judge,
The truth and which remarks are fudged."
She laughed and said to my surprise,
"It matters not if truth or lies,
Are laid before our very eyes.
What matters is a deep respect,
That everyone is different, yet,
Not one of us deserves the right,
To judge who's wrong or judge who's right."

An Almighty Word

This day is almost ending,
   And so I leave to you,
A word that will encourage you,
In everything you do.

This word will solve your problems,
This word will make you strong,
And those you have rejected,
From this word, they will belong.

This word we use in bed at night,
When asking from the heavens.
So charity that's well received,
Must also then be given.

This word applies to everyone,
No matter what they've done.
On using this I must insist,
Much better you'll become.

One wondrous day,
This word will say;
No wars, no hate, no greed.
But such a mighty word as this,
Is difficult to seed.

Though difficult to say,
It's quite impossible to live,
Within a world that's peaceful,
And not learn the word – forgive.

I Don't Believe

"I don't believe in God," she said,
"The notion is absurd and yet,
I like the words of Buddha, Christ,
The Merlin and Mohammed's life.

It's such a shame they all were wrong,
For even songs in churches sung,
Do fill my heart with utter bliss.
I really wish he did exist.

This fantasy he loves us all,
And help will come from just a call,
Remains as just a perfect dream,
About a world I've never seen."

"Dear Bat, I've listened to your sobs,
Can I now give you my response.
Alone you live on darkest shelf,
Believing only in yourself.

A flower grows when bathed in light,
And so will you, if this seems right.
So stretch your wings towards the sun,
And let abundance surely come.

Trust just your heart to find the truth,
For trust is not requiring proof.
Because my frightened little bat,
Trusting has to be like that."

Pleiades

The silver stallion stands alone,
As breeze does tease the hair that flows,
About his proud and thoughtful face,
A graceful son of noble race.

A loyal friend he's been to me,
And teacher too of dignity.
His kindly eye reminds us all,
Both strength and beauty's possible.

Against the clear November night,
The silent stars give guiding light.
How blessed am I and kind of Thee,
My guide should be the Pleiades.

Part II

His father was a Pluto,
  And from there, would come his name.
For he was just a yearling when,
The lives of ours would change.

And if he had competed then,
A duckling would have won.
But as the hands of time revealed,
My duckling was a swan.

The stars would soon be shining,
So I waited for the sun.
Yet starlit skys are old and cold,
And he's my dearest chum.

And so his names are many,
Kindness, dignity and grace.
Though documented in the sky,
My stallion has a place.

For Moses, Christ, a single star,
He crafted from the heavens.
But God agreed for Pleiades,
The stars that shine are seven.

The Stranger

Today I saw a puzzled face,
  Who said he came from outer space.
He says the Universe is vast,
But someone shouted, "Move your craft."

He spoke of having better days,
Just sailing past the Milky Way.
When even comets huge and fast,
Would still avoid conflicting paths.

He asked me why a rudeness grows,
From eating meat and wearing clothes.
I made it clear that some of us,
Can eat our meat without a fuss.
Yet from the mouths of whom he speaks,
Their case for greed and fear was weak.

He did receive one compliment,
Concerning an experiment.
And then refused their nervous charms,
Preferring just to keep his arms.

He said that people on this earth,
Do not appreciate the worth,
Of such abundant pleasant ground,
Compared to other souls around.

This news he gave was rather sad,
I said that few were very bad.
And on this point he did agree,
Though years would pass until they see.

It always takes a stranger's words,
Before the voice of reason's heard.
Yet now is not the time to speak,
While prejudice prefers to creep.

The Rat

"I do not like that silly book,
French tapestries, or way you look.
Your melba toast has strands of hair,
Attached to meat that still is rare.

The tea is weak, the cheese too strong,
Apart from that, there's nothing wrong.
And though you think I just complain,
I hope it doesn't rain again.

The reason why I said hello,
My brother's locked me out below.
What slime commits a crime like that,
To such an easy going rat?

Your whiskers need a liberal trim,
That coat is dull and tail's too thin.
And though you think you're always right,
I'm also free tomorrow night."

Sleep

Clear water from a spring's divine,
Norwegian prawns are very fine.
But even signs of being fed,
Do not compare with thoughts of bed.

The woollen womb that keeps me warm,
Strange places where I've never gone.
The distant sound of wind and rain,
I love them all the very same.

On nights when sleep is merely faked,
As worry worm is still awake.
And counting sheep just doesn't work,
I use this trusted little verse:

I thank you God for giving me,
My food and loving company.
Take special care of all my friends,
And help me too, to make amends.
Please teach me to be strong and kind,
Let me forgive all faults I find.
My love for you I'll always keep,
So would you Lord – just help me sleep.

The Ghost of Man

"Dear Lord I have a question,
I wish to understand.
In life I was a holy man,
But put to death a man.

He said he was the Son of God,
A bad and blasphemous thing.
So was I right to kill this man,
Or was this man a king?"

"Every man that walks the earth,
Is born a son of mine.
And every woman given birth,
Is from the womb divine.

And yes, the Man you talk about,
Was destined as a king.
But no one has the right to take,
The life from anything."

"How can a man be made the same,
As flesh of Holy Son?
For God is pure and man is flawed,
How can this thing be done?"

"The steps you take within your life,
Determine who you'll be.
So living life as if the Christ,
Will bring you close to me."

"This thing you ask,
Can not be done,
And so I'll say goodbye."

"Then let me ask this thing of you,
My son, just simply try."

Timmy's Gloves

Father Christmas had a stocking,
 Though you may be quite aghast,
To learn that every Christmas,
It lay empty on the hearth.

This year he said, "I'll find the time,
To fill it up a little.
A small cigar, a generous jar,
Of special yellow pickle."

"But first," he said, " I must address,
The reason why I'm here.
For giving not receiving,
Is what Christmas means each year.

I must remember Timmy's gran,
He says she's very old.
A pair of gloves he said she'd like,
Because she feels the cold.

Now what about young Timmy,
He's a tricky one to help,
As never will he ask of me,
A present for himself.

Samantha says she loves to sing,
And could she have a harp.
The twins said bring just anything,
I need to make a start."

The air was clear and faintest hint,
Of snow flakes did descend.
And on the close of Christmas Eve,
His work did almost end.

"There's one more house we have to do,"
The reindeers understood.
Young Timmy's home stood all alone,
In Seven Ashes Wood.

Young Timmy's eyes were tightly closed,
As Santa left his gifts.
"I would have liked to speak to him,
If I could have a wish.

But I am Father Christmas,
And that really wouldn't do.
God bless you little Timmy,
There are few as good as you."

He slowly climbed upon his sleigh,
"Well that's another year.
The chance of finding pickle,
Or cigars are gone I fear."

Then Timmy's door did open,
And just running through the snow,
Was Timmy in his dressing gown,
His cheeks an orange glow.

"My granny made some pickles,
And she really hopes they'll do.
They're special yellow pickles,
Made especially for you."

Our Santa held them in his hand,
And then began to shake.
"I thank you little Timmy,
Father Christmas rarely takes."

The sleigh bells loudly jingled,
As he left the frosted wood.
And Timmy waved with both his arms,
As only Timmy would.

"I love you Father Christmas,
Thank you so much for my gloves."
"What need have I of pickles,
With the gift of Timmy's love."

Be careful what you wish for,
As there is little doubt,
That time will find you grateful, or,
You could have done without.

I Wish

I wish the birds from dawn to night,
Would always sing and never fight.

I wish the food that can be found,
Would freely spread itself around.

I wish the cuckoo understood,
The worthy joys of motherhood.

I wish the kindness crows can show,
Could be for every bird they know.

And only hungry herons fish,
I wish the world could be like this.

Christmas Eve

An opal glow shone round her face,
Her wings were white, her dress was lace.
And as she stared from laden tree,
The angel softly smiled at me.

The crystal bird chirped not at all,
The golden bells just wouldn't toll.
Toy soldier's crack of rifle fire,
Was only heard from sparking pyre.

But as the clock's twelfth chime did ring,
The angel thus began to sing.
"Rejoice, for there is much to please us,
Happy Birthday, dearest Jesus."

The present — a final thought

Those gifts accepted long ago,
By rights — are no more pleasant,
Than jewels of wisdom offered now,
That sparkle in the present.

The author and artist, Lucian Eyers is the eldest of ten children and was born in Buckinghamshire in 1961. He was writing poetry, painting and drawing from childhood into adulthood. He read his first Sparky adventure book to thousands of children throughout England.

Lucian's spiritual poems tackle complex issues with clarity and wisdom. He explains that much of the inspiration and guidance for his poetry comes directly from his angel and spirit guides. Lucian has the rare ability to combine art and poetry that bring to the reader, laughter, hope and revelation.

Other titles by Lucian Eyers include:

THE SPARKY BOOK OF HOURS

SPARKY AND THE MAGIC GARDEN